IVONA,

Princess of Burgundia

Photo from the Jorge Lavelli production, Venice Festival, 1965.
(Courtesy Giacomelli Photographs.)

IVONA,

Princess of Burgundia

————— by Witold Gombrowicz

Translated from the Polish by Krystyna Griffith-Jones
and Catherine Robins

Grove Press, Inc., New York

Originally published as *Iwona, księżniczka Burgunda* in Warsaw in the Polish-language review *Skamander* in 1938.

This translation was first published in Great Britain by Calder and Boyars.

Library of Congress Catalog Card Number: 68-17730
First Grove Press Edition 1970
First Printing

Manufactured in the United States of America

────────AUTHOR'S NOTE

Ivona, Princess of Burgundia *is* Witold Gombrowicz's *first play. Written in 1935, it was published in the literary review* Skamander, *preceded by the following summary by the author.*

Act I: Prince Philip gets engaged to unappealing Ivona, for his dignity is offended by the girl's unattractiveness. Moreover, being a free spirit, he will not allow himself to come under the sway of the natural repulsion that this disagreeable person inspires in people. King Ignatius and Queen Margaret accept their son's engagement for fear of the scandal that Philip threatens to cause if they refuse.

Act II: It so happens that Ivona falls in love with the Prince. Surprised by this love, the Prince feels obliged to respond to it as a human being and as a man. He would like to love her in return.

Act III: The presence of Ivona at the Court causes strange complications. The Prince's engagement gives rise to jokes and gossip. The silence, the unsociability, the passivity of Ivona put the royal family in a difficult situation. Her natural lack of charm sets off dangerous associations of ideas, everyone finding in it a sort of reflection of his own imperfections or those of others.

An epidemic of unwholesome laughter strikes the Court.

The King remembers his sins of other days. The Queen, a secret scribbler, can no longer hide from herself the horror that her own poems inspire in her: she discovers that they resemble Ivona.

Absurd suspicions arise. There is worse stupidity and nonsense as each day goes by. Everyone feels this. The Prince is quite aware of it too, but does not know what to do about it: *he feels his position with Ivona is absurd too.* So how can he protect himself? He believes he has found an effective way of parading his feelings: he publicly embraces a lady of the Court and gets engaged to her, after having broken with Ivona. But a real break is impossible: the Prince knows that Ivona will always think of him, that she will have her own mental picture of the happiness of the young couple. Ivona has a hold over him. He decides to kill her.

Act IV: The King, the Chamberlain, the Queen, and the Prince each try to kill Ivona. But killing her outright is beyond them: the act seems too stupid, too absurd; there is no precise reason to justify it; every convention is against it.

The bestiality, the savagery, the stupidity, and the nonsense grow continually worse. On the advice of the Chamberlain, they decide to organize the murder and at the same time keep up all the appearances of majesty, of elegance, of superiority . . . it will be a murder "from above," not "from below." The undertaking is successful. The royal family is once again at peace.

W. G.
—*Translated by Helen R. Lane*

Originally published in Warsaw in 1938, *Ivona, Princess of Burgundia* was first staged by Jorge Lavelli for the Venice Festival, 1965, and subsequently transferred to the Théâtre de France in Paris. Since then it has been performed at the Royal Theater, Stockholm (1965), the Forum Theater, Berlin (1966), the Theatre Centrum, Rotterdam (1967), and the Theater am Neumarkt, Zurich (1968).

IVONA

KING IGNATIUS

QUEEN MARGARET

PRINCE PHILIP, *heir to the throne*

LORD CHAMBERLAIN

ISOBEL, *lady in waiting*

SIMON, *friend of the Prince*

CYPRIAN

Ivona's AUNTS

INNOCENT, *a courtier*

CHECKERS, *a servant*

BEGGAR

State Dignitaries, Courtiers, etc.

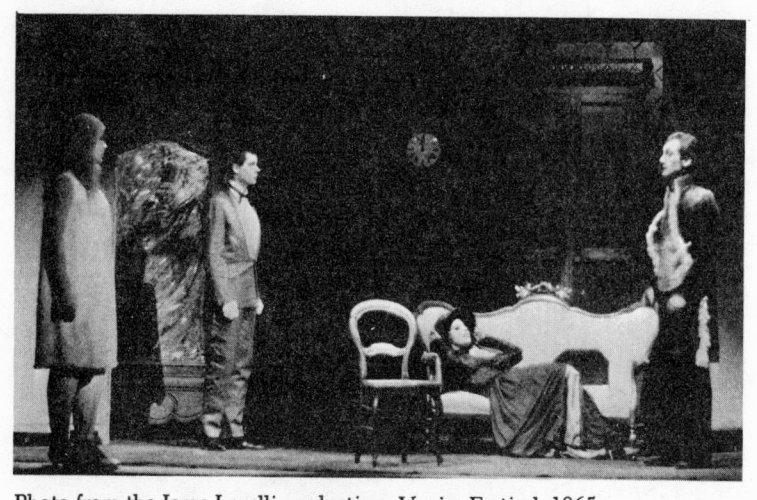

Photo from the Jorge Lavelli production, Venice Festival, 1965.
(Courtesy Giacomelli Photographs.)

IVONA,
Princess of Burgundia

─────────ACT ONE

The promenade—usual seats, trees, etc. The public in their Sunday best. Enter KING IGNATIUS, QUEEN MARGARET, PRINCE PHILIP, LORD CHAMBERLAIN, SIMON, *and* CYPRIAN *followed by ladies and gentlemen of the Court.*

QUEEN: What a wonderful sunset!

CHAMBERLAIN: Wonderful indeed, Your Majesty.

QUEEN: Truly inspiring, is it not?

CHAMBERLAIN: Exactly so, Madame, exactly.

KING: A wonderful sunset now and a lovely hand of bridge later . . . eh?

CHAMBERLAIN: Indeed. How perfectly Your Majesty combines an innate sense of beauty with a natural desire for the game.

A BEGGAR *approaches.*

What do you want?

BEGGAR: Help, my lord!

KING: My Lord Chamberlain, give him a crown. Let the people know that we have their welfare at heart.

QUEEN: Give him two. For the wonderful sunset.

LADIES: Aah!

KING: Give him three. Let's do it in style.

COURTIERS: Aah. Aah.

BEGGAR: God bless Your Majesty. May the Almighty bless your gracious Majesty, and your gracious Majesty bless the Almighty. (*Exit singing a beggar's song.*)

KING: Right now! Let's go. It won't do to be late for dinner. We've still got to make a tour of the gardens to mingle freely with our loyal subjects. It isn't a National Day for nothing, eh?

All get ready to go except PRINCE PHILIP.

You're not coming, Philip?

PHILIP (*picking up a newspaper off the ground*): Just a moment . . .

KING: Aha, I see. A rendezvous, eh? I was just the same at your age! Let's leave him to it. (*Exit chuckling.*)

QUEEN (*reproachfully*): Ignatius!

The trumpets sound, the Court leaves except the PRINCE, SIMON, *and* CYPRIAN.

CYPRIAN *and* SIMON: That affair, what a crushing bore!

PHILIP: Wait, let me read today's horoscope. (*Reading.*) "From twelve till two" . . . this isn't it . . . here it is. "Between seven and nine in the evening great expansion of vitality, growth of personality, excellent if hazardous ideas. This is the time for bold plans and for daring enterprise—"

CYPRIAN: What use is that to us?

PHILIP (*continues reading*): "—also for the affairs of the heart."

SIMON: Ah, that is different. (*Pointing to some passing girls.*) And there they are.

CYPRIAN: Let's go! Duty calls.

PHILIP: What do you mean—duty?

CYPRIAN: Action, action! We are young, we are men. Let us *be* young men and give work to the clergy so that they can *be* clergy. That's what I call proper division of labor.

SIMON: Look at that elegant and seductive siren. And the legs!

PHILIP: Oh, no. Not again? Not the same old thing?

CYPRIAN: No? But why not? Of course, again and again. What would she think if we just let her pass?

PHILIP: No.

SIMON: What? What do you mean "no"?

CYPRIAN (*with astonishment*): Doesn't it give Your Highness a glorious sense of achievement to hear some sweet lips say "yes," even if it means hearing the same old thing over and over again?

PHILIP: Of course, it does. Of course. (*Continues reading.*) "These hours favor the success of great undertakings, they bring refinement of feelings, they can be dangerous for those of exalted ambition and with an acute sense of dignity. Affairs started at this time may turn out to be successful or otherwise." At least that's true . . .

Enter ISOBEL.

Welcome, Madame.

CYPRIAN: This is an unexpected pleasure . . .

SIMON: A delight . . .

ISOBEL: Good evening, Your Highness. What are you doing here, away from the Court?

PHILIP: Exactly what I should be doing: while the presence of my father inspires the hearts of our loyal men I am here to inspire delicious dreams in the hearts of our ladies . . . but you, shouldn't you be attending the Queen?

ISOBEL: I am late. I am rushing there now. I have been for a walk.

PHILIP: You are in a rush? Where to?

ISOBEL: Your Highness seems a little distrait? Your voice sounds melancholy. Aren't you enjoying life any more, Your Highness? I am, to the full.

PHILIP: So am I. That's why . . .

CYPRIAN ⎫
SIMON ⎬ What?
ISOBEL ⎭

PHILIP: Humph . . .

CYPRIAN ⎫
SIMON ⎬ That's why what?
ISOBEL ⎭

PHILIP: Oh, nothing.

ISOBEL: Nothing? Are you not well, Your Highness?

SIMON: A cold?

CYPRIAN: Migraine?

PHILIP: Wrong, wrong again! I am seething, I tell you, throbbing and bubbling inside.

CYPRIAN (*staring at a girl*): Not bad, that blonde. Not at all bad.

PHILIP: Blonde? If you said brunette it would be exactly the same. (*Looking around, depressed.*) Trees and more trees, they are all exactly the same. I want something to happen.

SIMON: Look, another one.

CYPRIAN: Chaperoned!

SIMON: Two aunts!

Enter IVONA *and* AUNTS.

ISOBEL: What is this game?

CYPRIAN: Look, Your Highness, look. Oh, what an apparition! (*Laughter.*)

SIMON: Be quiet. Let's listen.

FIRST AUNT: Let's sit down. Can you see those young men, my child?

IVONA *is silent.*

Do smile, my child, always smile.

IVONA *is silent.*

SECOND AUNT: Why is your smile so apathetic, child? Why can't you smile properly?

IVONA *is silent.*

Yesterday again you had no success whatsoever. No success today, no success tomorrow. Why are you so unattractive, my child? Unglamorous, unseductive.

Nobody ever looks at you. You are a creature sent to try us, that's what you are.

FIRST AUNT: We have spent all our savings to buy this dress for you. You can't blame us for not trying . . .

CYPRIAN: The monstrous scarecrow!

ISOBEL: "Monstrous" is going a little far.

SIMON: Look at her! She dares to look.

CYPRIAN: The miserable wretch, the cry baby. Come, let's show her how despicable she is. We'll snub her, put her in her place.

SIMON: Yes, let's deflate this puffed-up misery. This is our appointed duty. You first, I'll follow.

They march in front of IVONA, *bursting into laughter under her nose.*

CYPRIAN: Ha, ha, ha, right under her nose.

ISOBEL: Oh, leave her alone. It's just silly.

FIRST AUNT (*to* IVONA): You see what you have let us in for?

SECOND AUNT: To be a public laughingstock. Oh, you are a trial. I thought that in my old age, when I ceased to be a woman, I would cease to be a butt of ridicule. Now I am old and as ridiculous as ever. Why? Just because of you.

CYPRIAN: Do you hear? The aunts are at it too. Go on! Give it to her!

SECOND AUNT: They are laughing at us again. If we leave now, they will laugh behind our backs. But if we stay, they will laugh in our faces.

FIRST AUNT: My child, last night at the dance, why didn't you even lift a finger?

SECOND AUNT: Why will nobody take any interest in you? Do you think we like it? Such sexual ambition as we ever had we have passed on to you and you do nothing; you don't even ski.

FIRST AUNT: Why don't you try pole vaulting? Other girls do . . .

CYPRIAN: Oh, look at the jellyfish. She makes me squirm, sets me on edge. She annoys me more than I can say. I can't bear it. I'm going to throw them off their seat, shall I?

SIMON: No—it isn't really worth the trouble. It would do just as well to shake your finger or to wave your hand or do anything else for that matter. Whatever you do to her turns into a snub. (*Sniffs.*)

SECOND AUNT: Look, now they're sniffing at us.

ISOBEL: Do leave her alone.

CYPRIAN: No, don't. Let's play a real joke on her. I'll pretend I'm maimed, I have a club foot, and it will make her think that not even the lamest dog would deign to lick the crumbs thrown from her table. (*Moves toward* IVONA.)

PHILIP: Stop. I have a much better idea.

CYPRIAN: I withdraw and leave the field to you.

SIMON: What's the idea? You look as if you were on to something this time.

PHILIP: More than you think. (*Approaches the* AUNTS.) Will you allow me to introduce myself? I am His Highness, Prince Philip, the heir to the throne.

AUNTS: Aah!

PHILIP: Ladies, you seem to be having trouble with this young person. Why is she so apathetic?

FIRST AUNT: It is our misfortune. She is suffering from an organic deficiency, from sluggishness of the blood.

SECOND AUNT: It causes her to swell in winter and to stink in summer. She has catarrh in the autumn and headaches in the spring.

PHILIP: It must make it difficult to choose the right season for anything. Is there no cure for her?

FIRST AUNT: The doctors say that if she were to become livelier, her blood would flow faster and then she might be cured.

PHILIP: But why doesn't she get livelier?

FIRST AUNT: Because her blood is too sluggish.

PHILIP: You mean if she became livelier her blood would flow faster and if her blood would flow faster she would become livelier. Most peculiar, a truly vicious circle. Do you know what I think . . .

SECOND AUNT: Your Highness is laughing at us of course. You are welcome to, I am sure.

PHILIP: Laughing at you? No, I am not laughing at all.

The clock strikes seven.

It is a grave time. Don't you feel a certain expansion of vitality, a growth of personality, a kind of ecstasy even?

FIRST AUNT: I'm afraid not. A little chilly, perhaps?

PHILIP: Odd. (*To* IVONA.) Don't you feel anything?

IVONA *is silent.*

SECOND AUNT: What could she possibly feel?

PHILIP: Do you know that the moment one looks at you, one is tempted to harm you in some way? To tie you up with a rope for instance and then to run at full speed or to drive you as a sort of milk cart. I would like to prick you with a pin and to make silly faces at you. You get on everybody's nerves. Don't you see you are like a red rag to a bull. You are provoking, you incense everyone, you drive people to distraction. Everyone has his personal irritant, but you are the universal irritant. The way you sit, the way you fiddle with your fingers and wiggle your toes. It's quite incredible. It's splendid in a way, a revelation of sorts. How do you manage to do it?

IVONA *is silent.*

It is your silence, the way you look offended. The sublime air of a proud queen. You are disdainful, you are soured—arrogance and vinegar. I recognize that for everyone there is, somewhere, somebody capable of firing them to a white heat; you do that to me, you must be mine, you shall be mine. Simon, Cyprian . . .

SIMON *and* CYPRIAN *draw nearer.*

Let me introduce you to this offended queen, this proud Anaemia. Look, her lips are moving. She would say something spiteful, if only she could think of something to say.

ISOBEL: How ridiculous. (*Draws nearer.*) Do leave her alone. It isn't funny and it's becoming most distasteful.

PHILIP (*sharply*):   Did you ever think it wouldn't be?

CYPRIAN: Allow me to introduce myself: I am Count Acidosis.

SIMON: Ha, ha, ha. I am Baron Leukemia. The joke is perhaps not subtle but certainly appropriate.

ISOBEL: Haven't you had enough? Leave the wretched creature alone.

PHILIP: Wretched? Not so fast, dear lady. What would you say if I told you that I was going to marry this wretched creature?

CYPRIAN *and* SIMON: Ha, ha, ha.

PHILIP: This is not a laughing matter. I may marry her . . .

SIMON *and* CYPRIAN *laugh*.

I will marry her. I simply have to. She is my turmoil. I will marry her. (*To the* AUNTS.) I may have your permission, mayn't I?

SIMON: It is you who are going too fast and too far with this joke. It won't be funny if they sue you for breach of promise.

PHILIP: A joke? And isn't she herself a colossal joke? Can't I be a joke as well? The balance is perfect: I am a prince; she is a proud and affronted queen. Just look at her. (*To* IVONA.) Madame, may I be allowed to request your hand in marriage?

FIRST AUNT: Good gracious.

SECOND AUNT: Good gracious. Your Highness has a generous heart.

FIRST AUNT: Your Highness is a true philanthropist.

CYPRIAN: Incredible.

SIMON: Mad. I beg you in the name of your ancestors.

CYPRIAN: I beg you in the name of your descendants.

PHILIP: Stop, both of you. (*Takes Ivona's hand.*)

ISOBEL: The King.

CYPRIAN: The King.

SIMON: The King.

Trumpets, trumpets, etc. Enter the KING, *the* QUEEN, *the* LORD CHAMBERLAIN, *followed by ladies and gentlemen of the Court.*

AUNTS: We better make ourselves scarce before the storm breaks. (*They flee.*)

KING: Still here, Philip? I see you are amusing yourself. (*To his entourage.*) Didn't I tell you? My own flesh and blood.

QUEEN: Ignatius.

KING: I told you, eh! What did I say? Blood runs thicker than water, like father like son, eh! (*Aside.*) Good Lord, this nymph seems a little . . . ? What is this frump, my son?

PHILIP: Allow me, Sir, to present my future wife.

KING: Your what?

ISOBEL: His Highness is joking, of course.

KING: Joking—now I see. Just like his father. Practical jokes are about the only thing I still enjoy these days. The funny thing is, the older the joke, the more it pleases me. I really don't know why. There are no

jokes like the old jokes, eh! The older they are, the younger they make me feel.

CHAMBERLAIN: Exactly so, Your Majesty. May I concur with your judgment. Nothing is more rejuvenating than a really ancient joke.

QUEEN (*embarrassed*): Philippe . . .

PHILIP: This is not a joke.

QUEEN: What is it then, Philippe, if it's not a joke . . .

PHILIP: It is my betrothal.

KING: What!!!

The Court flee in panic.

QUEEN: We must keep our temper at all cost. We must proceed with tact. (*To* IVONA.) Would you mind looking at that tree over there. (*To* PRINCE PHILIP.) Philippe, you are putting her in an impossible position. You are putting us in an impossible position, you are putting yourself in an impossible position. You are creating an impossible situation all round. (*To the* KING.) Calmly, Ignatius, calmly.

PHILIP: Your Majesties, I see that in your eyes I have done something outrageous. That I, the Prince of the blood, should be linked to a person like this . . .

KING: Now you are talking sense.

PHILIP: I don't see it like that at all. I am not taking her because I have too little, but because I have too much. Surely this is not wrong, and I am not lowering myself.

KING: Too little? Too much? What do you mean "too much"?

PHILIP: Am I not rich enough to take on this misery? Why, pray, should only prettiness attract me? Who says so? What is wrong with being ugly? Is there a law against it? Even if there were, I would not follow it blindly. I am free.

KING: You can't be serious, Philip. Pride has gone to your head. Why must you muddle quite simple things? You meet a pretty girl, you like her, you naturally . . . eh? If she isn't pretty, on the other hand, you just as naturally run as fast as you can. There is nothing complicated about it, it is the law of nature. As for myself (*a cautious glance at the* QUEEN), I follow it willingly, to be sure.

PHILIP: This law of nature seems to me stupid, vulgar, ridiculous, and unjust.

CHAMBERLAIN: It must be so, if you say so, Sir, but all the same the most stupid laws of nature are the most delectable, Your Highness.

KING: Are you bored, Philip? Are you weary of your studies at the College of Advanced Furnace Construction? What about your splendid welfare work among our poorer subjects?

QUEEN: And all your childish games—tennis, bridge, polo? And football, and dominoes?

CHAMBERLAIN: Is it possible, if I may be allowed to put it somewhat plainly, that it is that very freedom of sexual behavior among your contemporaries which is the cause of your ennui, Your Highness? It is a little hard to believe, I must admit. I don't think it would have bored me.

PHILIP: To hell with sexual freedom. I am going to marry, that's all.

KING: To marry. To marry, indeed. You damnable insolent puppy. I'll teach you to laugh at us, I'll cast you out.

QUEEN: Ignatius, you couldn't do that.

KING: I will do it. I will lay a curse on him. I will put him in irons. I will throw him out into the street.

QUEEN: Ignatius, oh, Ignatius. It would cause such a scandal. Ignatius, he is only doing it out of the goodness of his heart.

KING: Out of the goodness of his heart, indeed! He is breaking his old father's heart.

QUEEN: He is doing it out of pity. He has always been so susceptible and the misfortune of this miserable girl must have affected him deeply. Oh, Ignatius, it would cause such a scandal if you did anything rash.

KING (*suspiciously*):   Her misfortune has affected him? Is that what you think?

CHAMBERLAIN: Your Majesty, the Queen is so right. His Highness is doing it entirely out of his natural generosity. It is a generous deed, a noble deed. (*Aside to the* KING.) Don't you see, Sire, unless we call it a generous deed, it is a scandalous one as surely as two and two make four. You know, Sire, how obstinate Prince Philip is. We must avoid scandal at all cost.

KING: Yes! Well, well . . . on second thought we have to admit that your action was well intentioned. Although very, very rash, of course, eh? Generosity, that's it. Generosity!

PHILIP: It isn't generosity at all.

QUEEN (*talking very fast*): But it is, it is. Philippe, dear, do not interrupt. We know best. (*Solemnly.*) In recognition of your goodness we will allow you to present your fiancée to us. The way she bears misfortune has appealed to our best, most refined feelings. It has indeed affected us deeply. We will receive her at the palace as one equal to the highest in the land. This, we are sure, will not bring discredit on our house, but indeed exalt it.

PHILIP (*interrupts*): Simon, send her here; Their Majesties have consented.

QUEEN: Ignatius, calm, remember!

PHILIP (*approaches, leading* IVONA *on his arm. The* COURTIERS *emerge from under the trees. Trumpets, trumpets, etc.*): Your Majesties, may I be allowed to present my fiancée?

CHAMBERLAIN (*in a whisper*): Curtsy. Curtsy.

IVONA *does nothing.*

Curtsy, curtsy.

PHILIP: Curtsy.

QUEEN: Here, here. (*She bows slightly to give* IVONA *a hint.*) Now ... now.

KING *bows slightly, as the* QUEEN *has just done.*

IVONA *does nothing.*

PHILIP (*a little perplexed*): This is the King, my father, His Majesty, and this is the Queen, my mother, Her Majesty. Curtsy. Curtsy.

IVONA *does nothing.*

QUEEN (*hurriedly*): Philippe, my dear, we are touched. The sweet creature. (*Kisses* IVONA.) My child, we will be mother and father to you, we are delighted with the truly evangelical spirit of our son, we respect his choice. Philippe, no retreat! Upward and onward forever.

CHAMBERLAIN: *Aah, quel sentiment recherché!*

COURTIERS (*on a signal from the* CHAMBERLAIN): Aah!

KING (*absolutely blank*): Upward . . . onward . . . I suppose you could put it like that.

QUEEN (*continues hurriedly*): Now take her in and have her apartments made ready. See that she lacks nothing.

CHAMBERLAIN: Aah!

COURTIERS: Aah!

Exit PRINCE PHILIP, IVONA, SIMON, *and the* COUTRIERS.

KING: Oh, oh, she . . . we . . . damn . . . my goodness me, do you see what happened? In the end we had to bow to her . . . she wouldn't . . . and she didn't . . . ugh. Isn't she a horror!

QUEEN: Isn't she? That is the beauty of his deed.

CHAMBERLAIN: Quite so, Your Majesty, quite so. If I may coin a phrase: the uglier the betrothed, the more beautiful the betrothal. Sire, the Prince will get over it in a few days if we don't force the issue. I will see him today to find out what his intentions are. It's just an extravaganza and we must not cross him in any way, if we don't want to make things worse. We must

keep our peace, watch our step, and proceed with caution.

QUEEN: And tact, Ignatius, and tact.

They leave.

————ACT TWO

The Prince's apartments. Enter PRINCE PHILIP, SIMON, IVONA. CHECKERS, *duster in hand, comes in through opposite door.*

PHILIP: Out of the way, Checkers.

CHECKERS *leaves.*

Make her sit down. I am still afraid she may run away. Should we tie her to the table leg?

SIMON: She's half dead, she won't run. Philip . . .

PHILIP: Well?

SIMON (*disapproving*): Why are you doing this, Philip?

PHILIP: Why? Why? Don't you see that she is my dragon to be slain, my Gordian knot to be cut? I am a hunter in the night, singlehanded after a lion. I am Theseus taking the bull by the horns. Simon—

SIMON: One can't get any sense out of you.

PHILIP: Or it may be just irresistible curiosity. Rather as if one were prodding a worm with a stick to see if it will turn.

SIMON: Will you let me tell you what I think?

PHILIP: Do.

SIMON: Let us leave her alone. In half an hour's time we won't know what to do with her. It will be very inconvenient apart from anything else. You were far too rash.

PHILIP: I thought both you and Cyprian were rash enough with her.

SIMON: Quite true, we were. But it is one thing to have a little joke in the open air and a far different thing to drag her into the castle. My advice is to let her go at once.

PHILIP: Look at the way she sits. Incredible! All the same, what impertinence. Just because this girl is as she is, must one assume that she can't attract anyone at all? Infernal cheek on the part of nature. (*Looks at* IVONA.) Do you know, it is only since I first set eyes on her that I have really felt . . . no, that I have become truly a prince. Before that I felt no more than a baron and one of the lesser ones at that.

SIMON: How very odd. I would have said the opposite is the case. Since you saw her you have behaved more like a commoner than a prince.

PHILIP: It is odd but I must tell you that I have never felt so self-assured, so splendid, so brilliant. Tra-la. (*Places a pen upside down on the end of his finger.*) Look, I could never do this before. Apparently, it is necessary to find someone completely inferior to appreciate one's own excellence. To be a prince in name is nothing. To be a prince in essence—it's heaven, it's pure joy. I am floating on air. (*He dances around the room.*) Now let us have a look at our splendid folly, our magnificent

distraction. Madame, could you be prevailed upon to speak?

IVONA *is silent.*

You know, it is not that she's wholly ugly; it is that element of misery within her composition.

SIMON: That is the worst of it.

PHILIP: Madame, why are you like this?

IVONA *is silent.*

Silence, silence, why are you like this?

IVONA *is silent.*

SIMON: No answer. Offended.

PHILIP: Offended.

SIMON: Perhaps not offended. Just scared.

PHILIP: A little overwhelmed?

IVONA (*quietly and uneasily*): Please, leave me alone. I am not offended.

PHILIP: Not offended, then why don't you answer?

IVONA *is silent.*

Well?

IVONA *is silent.*

Can't you? Why?

IVONA *is silent.*

SIMON: Ha, ha, ha! She can't. She is feeling offended after all.

PHILIP: Madame, please, be kind enough to explain to us

your mechanism. You are not all that stupid. Why then do people treat you as if you could not tell black from white. Are they just teasing you?

SIMON: She isn't stupid, she's in a stupid situation.

PHILIP: You are right. I beg your forgiveness. Look, Simon, isn't it amazing? Her nose is well proportioned, and she is not brainless. In fact, she is not a bit worse than many of the girls we know. But nobody would dream of teasing others as they tease you, would they? Why are you the scapegoat? Has it just become a habit?

IVONA (*quietly*): It is a wheel, it goes round and round in circles.

SIMON: What wheel?

PHILIP: Don't interrupt. What wheel?

IVONA: It is going round and round, always, everybody, everything, all the time.

PHILIP: Round and round? Why round? There is something mystical about it: a wheel? All circles are mystical. For example, she is lethargic. Why? Because she is out of sorts. And why is she out of sorts? Because she is lethargic, of course. Don't you see it is a circle? A vicious circle.

SIMON (*to* IVONA): It's your own fault, cheer up a little, you bumpkin.

IVONA *is silent.*

PHILIP: She dismissed you like a schoolboy, don't you see?

SIMON: Come now, pluck up courage. A little humor. A little life. Look, you are just sulking. Smile a little and all will be well.

PHILIP: Smile just a little. It won't hurt.

IVONA *is silent.*

She won't. She is quite right not to. It would be so out of keeping. It would only make things worse. She would be even more annoying, more irritating, more provoking, wouldn't she? Simon, I have never seen anything like it. Isn't it magnificent? What do you think would happen if we smiled at her first?

SIMON: It wouldn't work, it would be a pitying smile. A smile of pity wouldn't really do, would it?

PHILIP: Isn't it an absolutely hellish combination, an infernal dialectic. You can see, can't you, for all that she keeps silent as the grave, she herself has thought it all out. There is a method in it, it's a system, a *perpetuum mobile.* Inside everything is spinning, as if a mad dog were chasing its own tail, and outside, deathly stillness.

SIMON: A hermetic, self-contained system.

PHILIP: It couldn't have been like this always, though, could it? Not at the beginning? Why are you afraid? Because you are shy. But why are you shy? Because you are afraid, a little. Which came first? There must have been a beginning.

IVONA *is silent.*

Let me see. There must be something in you— something positive as it were, a spark. You can't consist only of deficiencies . . . There must be something, some reason, some quality, a mainstay of sorts. Something you like in yourself, that you believe in. I promise you, we will fan that spark into a blaze.

IVONA *is silent.*

Wait. This is important. Suppose someone comes up to you and tells you that you are a horror, an abomination, and a curse. Striking, wounding, killing words. What would you reply? Would you say: "Yes, I am all this, it's true, but . . ." But what? What would you say?

IVONA *is silent.*

SIMON: Come, tell us.

PHILIP: For instance, "But I am kindhearted" or "But I am nice." Don't you see? One positive quality, one virtue, is all we need.

SIMON (*violently*):   Do say something. Speak, Madame, speak.

PHILIP: Perhaps you write poetry: elegies, epitaphs? However bad they are I would recite them with enthusiasm, I swear. Oh, couldn't you give me just something to build on? Do you, in fact, write poetry?

IVONA *is silent.*

SIMON: She despises it.

PHILIP: Do you believe in God? Do you pray? Do you kneel? Do you believe that Christ Our Lord died on the Cross for you?

IVONA (*contemptuously*):   Yes.

PHILIP: A miracle. At last. Glory be to God. But why with such contempt? You can't speak with contempt about the God you believe in.

SIMON: It is beyond me.

PHILIP: I will tell you something, Simon. She only believes in God because of her deficiencies. She knows
that if she were like other people, she would not believe. She believes in God but she knows all the time
that God is only a sort of dressing to cover up her
psychosomatic sores. (*To* IVONA.) Isn't it so?

IVONA *is silent.*

Brrr! Even so, there is some appalling lethargic
wisdom in it.

SIMON: Medicine. Medicine. Pills and a suitable treat-
ment would cure that wisdom of hers. General hy-
giene, a morning walk, sports and games, rolls and
butter.

PHILIP: You forget her body does not assimilate medi-
cines. It does not do so because it is too sluggish, etc.,
etc. We know that sequence. It doesn't assimilate reme-
dies for sluggishness because it is too sluggish. You
are forgetting the mystic cycle. The morning walks
and games would of course cure her weakness but
she can't go for walks because she is too weak. Simon,
have you ever heard anything like it? It calls for pity,
but what a curious kind of pity . . .

SIMON (*to* IVONA): It must be a punishment for your
sins. You must have misbehaved prodigiously in your
childhood. Philip, there must be sin at the bottom
of this. It could not have happened without a monu-
mental lapse. You have sinned.

IVONA *is silent.*

PHILIP: Oh, at last I have grasped it—at last! Listen, if
you are so weak, then you must feel everything less

strongly, suffer less, less and less. Do you hear? The circle closes to your advantage, it all evens out. You know less of the fascination of the world, but it must also hurt you less.

IVONA *is silent.*

Well?

IVONA, *silent, glances furtively at* PRINCE PHILIP.

SIMON (*noticing*): What is she doing?

PHILIP: What?

SIMON: Nothing, really. Philip!

PHILIP (*getting anxious*): What is she doing?

SIMON: Philip. She is making eyes at you.

PHILIP: She couldn't . . .

SIMON: Look. She is. Positively. She is eating you up with her eyes. Passionately, damn it. She is squirming her way toward you. Take care. This weakness is lusting, seething with desire.

PHILIP: She's shameless, it is a scandal and a disgrace. How dare you fasten upon me? You worm, you maggot. Shall we roast her a little? Make a poker red-hot and make her dance?

SIMON: Philip, stop it.

PHILIP: There is something unbearable about her. I can't stand it. It's offensive. You are offending me. I do not wish to know about your troubles. You . . . pessimist! You . . . realist!

SIMON: Philip.

PHILIP: Look, how she is sitting . . .

SIMON: Make her get up.

PHILIP: Then she will be standing, and that will be even worse. Look at her—begging, begging for something . . . asking me. Simon, we must get rid of this creature. Give me a knife. I will cut her throat with pleasure.

SIMON: For God's sake!

PHILIP: I'm joking, of course. But she is scared. She is really scared—it's foul. Why are you frightened, Madame, when it was only a joke? It was a joke—why are you taking it seriously?

SIMON: Now you are overdoing it.

PHILIP: What? I suppose so. How funny, you really think I'm overacting. Very likely. But it's her fault, not mine. It is she and not I . . .

A bell. Enter CHECKERS.

SIMON: Who is that? (*Looks through the window.*) Visitors, I think. The Lord Chamberlain and some ladies.

CHECKERS: Should I open the door?

PHILIP: They've come to pry. Let us go and tidy ourselves.

PRINCE PHILIP, SIMON, *and* IVONA *leave the room.* CHECKERS *opens the door. Enter the* LORD CHAMBERLAIN, TWO GENTLEMEN, FOUR LADIES, *and* INNOCENT.

FIRST LADY: Nobody in? (*Looks around.*)

SECOND LADY: Oh, really, I can't. (*Giggles.*)

FIRST GENTLEMAN: And what if it is serious?

CHAMBERLAIN: Quiet, please, ladies. I beg you, no giggling.

LADIES *giggle.*

No giggling, I said. We must behave as if nothing has happened, if we are to find out how the wind is blowing.

FIRST LADY: And what if it is serious? Oh, what an idea. Look, her hat. What a hat! I can't! I have a stitch!

CHAMBERLAIN: A little self-control, I beg of you.

ALL GUESTS: But we can't. Stop or I will burst. Stop it. We are bursting. We are dying.

They are all laughing except INNOCENT. *Enter* PRINCE PHILIP, SIMON, *and* IVONA.

ALL GUESTS: Your Highness. (*Bow and curtsy.*)

CHAMBERLAIN: We were just passing. We couldn't refrain from calling . . . (*Rubs his hands.*) All of us.

PHILIP: Ivona, darling—I am delighted to be able to present you to my future wife.

GUESTS: Aah! (*Bowing.*) Congratulations, congratulations.

PHILIP: My dear, overcome your shyness and say something. These ladies and gentlemen belong to the best society. Don't be afraid of them as if they were cannibals or chimpanzees from Borneo. I apologize for my fiancée. She is exceptionally sensitive, proud, and shy— somewhat difficult to get on with. (*To* IVONA.) Do sit down, we can't be kept standing forever.

IVONA *moves as if to sit on the floor.*

SIMON: Oh, no, not there.

GUESTS: Ha, ha, ha, ha.

FIRST GENTLEMAN: Could have sworn there was a chair there.

FIRST LADY: There was, but it must have run away.

GUESTS: Ha, ha, ha. Magic. A bad omen.

CHAMBERLAIN: Please, sit down. (*Moves a chair nearer.*) Be careful, though.

SIMON: Hold it, so it doesn't run away again.

CHAMBERLAIN: Be kind enough to aim with care.

PHILIP: Aim well, my dear.

IVONA *sits down.*

Well done.

All take seats except PRINCE PHILIP.

FIRST LADY (*in an aside to* PRINCE PHILIP *with a certain degree of familiarity*):   Really, Your Highness. It's too much. I will die of laughter.

SECOND LADY (*in an aside to* PRINCE PHILIP):   I will burst. I will die. It is of course the most fashionable kind of practical joke. I didn't know Your Highness had such a flair for it. Only look at her!

PHILIP (*encouraging his* GUESTS):   Ha, ha, ha.

GUESTS: Ha, ha, ha.

PHILIP (*louder*):   Ha, ha, ha.

GUESTS (*louder*):   Ha, ha, ha.

PHILIP (*louder*):   Ha, ha, ha.

GUESTS (*not quite sure*): Ha, ha, ha, ha. (*Laughter dies out. Silence.*)

CHAMBERLAIN *coughs.*

FIRST LADY: I must leave, I'm afraid. I have just remembered an appointment. Your Highness will excuse me . . .

SECOND LADY: I have to go as well. Your Highness will forgive me, I have got an appointment too. (*In a low voice to* PRINCE PHILIP.) I understand now. You have arranged it all to show us up. What a joke! Your Highness gets engaged to this simpleton to make fools of us. Your Highness must have found out about Lady Joanna's face-lifts and wigs. That's why you got engaged to this peasant—to show her up. I can assure you that the irony of your stratagem has not escaped me. I take my leave.

PHILIP: The irony?

FIRST LADY (*who heard most of it, to* SECOND LADY): If it were intended to show up anybody it would be more likely you with your false teeth. (*To* PRINCE PHILIP.) Your Highness, do not be too cruel, I beg you! And now I really must be going.

SECOND LADY: My teeth. More likely your false bust.

FIRST LADY: What about your crooked shoulder?

SECOND LADY: Remember your toes.

GUESTS: We really must be going.

PHILIP: Don't go yet.

GUESTS: It is time, Your Highness. It's time for us to go.

The GUESTS *leave except* LORD CHAMBERLAIN *and* IN-
NOCENT. *One can hear from the stairs outside:* "toes,"
"teeth," "wig," *etc.*

CHAMBERLAIN: Forgive me, Your Highness, but I am
forced to request an immediate interview with you,
Sir. Your Highness has frightened our fair ladies away.

PHILIP: I did not, their own secrets have driven them
away. It appears that there is nothing more frighten-
ing. Famine and war are nothing compared to one
little, well-hidden false tooth.

INNOCENT: Excuse me.

PHILIP: What is this? You are still here?

INNOCENT: I am. I am sorry. I only wanted to say that
this is vile.

PHILIP: What is vile?

INNOCENT: Vile and mean. I am sorry. I must sit down.
Excitement always upsets my breathing.

PHILIP: You said something was vile?

INNOCENT: I am sorry . . . I got carried away. Forgive me,
Your Highness. Forget about it, please. I am sorry.
(*Wants to leave.*)

PHILIP: Wait. You said something was mean and vile.

INNOCENT (*his speech alternates between deadly quiet and
high irritation*): But I see now that I can't keep it
up.

CHAMBERLAIN: What a silly expression. Keep up what?

INNOCENT: Keep up what I have started. (*Wanting to
leave.*) I apologize.

PHILIP: Wait a moment, don't be so mysterious, Mister . . . Mister . . . Mister . . .

INNOCENT: I love her and that is why I got carried away and started protesting. But I withdraw my protest and I beg you to forget the whole incident.

PHILIP: You love her?

SIMON: Well, I'll be damned.

CHAMBERLAIN: How comic.

PHILIP: You pierce my heart. This is a grave matter. Do you know the sudden transition from frivolity to gravity? There is holiness in it. It's a revelation.

INNOCENT: Your Highness, I am a humble man.

PHILIP: Forgive me, Ivona. Thank God, somebody can love even you. So it is possible. You have got somebody who . . . What a relief. I have done what I have because I couldn't bear you, I couldn't bear the thought of you. Forgive me, I give you my blessing. Go now. Leave me alone.

SIMON (*looking at* IVONA, *who is bowing her head*): Crying!

PHILIP: Crying? It's happiness.

SIMON: I wouldn't trust the crybaby. Her sort cry only from unhappiness. Do you love him?

IVONA *is silent.*

It is a negative silence.

PHILIP: It doesn't matter. (*To* IVONA.) Things are not so bad, now that there is somebody who loves you. (*To* INNOCENT.) You are a brave person, a real man. Go on

loving her. It's splendid. You have redeemed us all, we are all indebted to you.

INNOCENT: Vanity prompts me to explain that she loves me too. She doesn't like to admit it in front of the Prince, naturally, as I don't gratify her pride. (*To* IVONA.) It isn't worth pretending, you have after all told me many times that you loved me.

IVONA *is silent.*

(*Irritated.*) Don't be so uppish. If you wish to know, you attract me just as little as I do you, or even less . . .

PHILIP: What?

INNOCENT (*calmly*): Allow me to explain, Your Highness. When I said I loved her, I meant that I loved her for want of something better, because of the absence, let us say, of . . .

CHAMBERLAIN: *Fi donc.* You mustn't speak like this.

INNOCENT: The point is that desirable women or even average women are so difficult and unbending. With her one can relax. There is no competition and no showing off. I relax with her and she with me. We love one another because she is as unattractive to me as I am to her, we are equal.

PHILIP: I admire your frankness.

INNOCENT: I would lie willingly but it would be useless. Everybody sees through everything these days. The fig leaves have become transparent. There is nothing left but to be honest. I am not denying that our love is a consolation prize. I have as much success with women as she with men. All the same I am jealous. I have a

right to show it. (*To* IVONA *with surprising passion.*)
You have fallen in love, haven't you? With him? Him?

IVONA (*cries out*):   Get out, go!

INNOCENT: Infatuated!

IVONA (*collapsing after her great effort*):   Go . . .

PHILIP: She spoke. But in that case . . . she spoke. You
heard. That means she really loves me.

INNOCENT: It's obvious. I have lost as usual. I shall go.
I am going. (*Exits.*)

PHILIP: She loves me. Instead of hating me. I am cruel
to her. I humiliate her. She falls in love with me and
now she loves me. Because I can't stand her, she loves
me. This is grave.

Enter CHECKERS.

Go away, Checkers. What should I do?

CHAMBERLAIN: If Your Highness could be a little more
lighthearted about it.

PHILIP: It can't be. Tell me you don't . . . you don't love
me?

IVONA *is silent.*

She loves me. I am loved by her. I am loved by
her. I am her beloved. I am involved with her. She
has enmeshed me. I can't look down on her if she
loves me. I cannot scorn from outside because I am
part of her. All this time I thought that I existed on
my own, by myself—and (*snaps his fingers*) she has
caught me. She is the trap and I am captured. You
love me, I must love you, I will love you.

bing?

o learn to love.

out?

at hot water he has
ladies came to her
ng that our son had
for a joke, just to
secrets, uhm . . .
If that's all he's

ity.

gly women turn
es.

is nothing more
generally assumed
s, but a really un-
a really unpleasant
especially when
ss is of proper, ah,
ung man who ap-
undue confidence
us capers.

My ladies are all
one too far.

e must take all

e loves her. I
ds. I can't say
all take cover

n't know anything
y experience of life
an must know noth-
e to be a gentleman

————ACT THREE

A room in the castle. SIMON *seated, two* LADIES *of the Court walk through, giggling, followed by* PRINCE PHILIP.

PHILIP: What are you doing?

SIMON: Sitting.

PHILIP: And what else?

SIMON: Nothing.

PHILIP: What were they talking and laughing about, the two bubbling blunderers? What were they saying?

SIMON: They were giggling. Women often do. It's their nature and it suits them best.

PHILIP: Were they laughing at me?

SIMON: Why should they? They were just laughing at each other.

PHILIP: If not at me, then at her . . . at my fiancée. But surely their laughter has changed? I may be wrong but it seems to me that they in fact no longer laugh at her but at me. Everyone is whispering and giggling. Is it a delusion? Do something for me. Try to find out what they are saying about us, what kind of ridicule

they are building up. I would like to know. It does not matter, of course, but I would like to know. You also might tell them that if they continue to take liberties behind my back . . .

SIMON: What is happening to you, Philip? You are as touchy and as easily hurt as your fiancée. You are not yourself.

PHILIP: Don't go too far. I have had enough. I am not used to being a laughingstock or to having my actions and my feelings ridiculed. Tell all of them that if anyone permits himself the least impropriety, the shadow of a slight . . .

The doors open, trumpets, etc. Enter the KING, the QUEEN, IVONA, and the LORD CHAMBERLAIN, ISOBEL, and the COURTIERS.

QUEEN (*to* IVONA): You liked it? You liked it, didn't you? Have you had enough? Sufficient? (*Smiles and kisses* IVONA *ingratiatingly.*) Perhaps another pear in syrup? A nice sweet one?

IVONA *is silent.*

It would do you good. So much good.

KING: Good. Good!

QUEEN: Perhaps a little cream? Cream does you good. It's so nutritious. What about some cream? Or milk? Milk with sugar?

Silence.

What is it? No appetite? Naughty, naughty. What are we going to do about it?

IVONA *is silent.*

SIMON: What are you going to do?

PHILIP: To start loving her!

SIMON: You can't do the impossible.

PHILIP (*to* IVONA): Ivona, put your hat on

SIMON *and* CHAMBERLAIN: Where are you g

PHILIP: For a walk. Just the two of us. T

PRINCE PHILIP and IVONA leave.

SIMON: What now?

CHAMBERLAIN: She has turned his head.

SIMON: How could she? This monstros

CHAMBERLAIN: Sometimes, you know, u heads more effectively than pretty on

SIMON: The mind boggles.

CHAMBERLAIN: I can tell you, there dangerous than an ugly woman. It is that agreeable women are dangerou pleasant woman—or, for a woman, man—truly unappetizing women. young and when the disagreeablene intensity . . . the inexperienced y proaches that sort of woman with may get involved in really monstr

SIMON: Monstrous capers?

CHAMBERLAIN: Young man, you d about it, and even I with all m don't. There are things a gentlem ing about, because he would ceas if he did.

CHAMBERLAIN: Nothing? (*Laughs benevolently.*) Nothing?

KING: Nothing? (*Laughs at first benevolently, then nervously.*) Nothing? (*To* LORD CHAMBERLAIN.) Nothing?

QUEEN: Nothing?

CHAMBERLAIN: Nothing at all, Your Majesty. In fact, if the truth be told, nothing.

Silence.

QUEEN: Such a shy creature. So nice, so quiet. If only she would say something occasionally. (*To* IVONA.) If you would say something sometimes, my pet. It is not difficult, really. One has to say something sometimes—for decency's sake. It's elementary decency. Surely you want to behave decently? What are we going to do now? How will we occupy ourselves?

KING: Well?

CHAMBERLAIN: Well?

IVONA *is silent.*

KING: What? Nothing, Surely it is impossible never to know the answer! You can't mope around the house all day, eh? And nothing, nothing, nil. It's such a bore, don't you see? (*He stares at them all in stupefaction.*) Say something, for goodness' sake.

CHAMBERLAIN: Heaven help us.

QUEEN: May the Lord have mercy upon us.

Enter CHECKERS.

CHECKERS: Your Highness, the doctor has arrived and is waiting in the gallery.

PHILIP (*to* IVONA): Come. You will excuse us. (PHILIP *and* IVONA *leave.*)

QUEEN: Philippe, just a moment . . . Philippe.

PHILIP *returns.*

(*To the* COURTIERS.) Will you leave us, please, we have to speak to our son.

The COURTIERS *leave.*

Philippe, you can't complain that we do not respect your feelings. We are like a mother and father to this poor child. But couldn't you use your influence to make her slightly more communicative? She hasn't said a word during tea, she hasn't said a word during lunch or breakfast for that matter. In fact, she has not said a word all day long. Just think what they all think of her, and of us. The decencies should be preserved, Philippe.

PHILIP (*sarcastically*): Decencies?

QUEEN: My dear son, aren't we offering her a mother's heart? We love her, with all her faults, because she loves you.

PHILIP (*threateningly*): You love her! Love! See to it that you do. (*He leaves.*)

QUEEN: O Lord, give us wisdom. O Lord, guide us. Ignatius, you are not showing her enough warmth; she is frightened of you.

KING: Frightened be damned. Then how does she manage to get into every corner and to look through every

window? She will use up all our windows in no time at all. And still not a word, nothing at all. Frightened, my foot. (*To* LORD CHAMBERLAIN.) Give me the reports. Ah, France is rising again. (*To himself.*) Frightened, but of what? Of me? (*To the* QUEEN.) And you are fussing around her too much. (*Imitates the* QUEEN.) "Another pear?" "Or another little cake?" As if you were a boardinghouse landlady.

QUEEN: You are not fussing, you are quite natural with her, aren't you? You only have to swallow every time you are about to speak to her, and you look scared whenever you are near her. Do you think that nobody has noticed?

KING: Scared? It's she who is scared. (*Murmurs.*) The viper.

CHAMBERLAIN: The majesty of Your Majesty seems to intimidate her. I am not the least surprised—I too have been intimidated myself on occasions. In fact, I have trembled at the sight of Your Majesty. May I be allowed to suggest that Your Majesty might encourage her a little: take her aside and have a little talk.

KING: With her? Me? With our Grumpy Dumpy? What . . .

QUEEN: A splendid idea. She needs encouragement. We must arrange little talks in private, à deux or à trois. When she gets used to us we will attempt it with the others. Ignatius, don't be churlish. We will start at once. I am going to send her to you under some pretext. Philippe is with the doctor. I know! I will send her back for some wool. But I beg you, promise to behave like a true father to her. (*Leaves.*)

KING: Lord Chamberlain, look what you've got me into. What can I talk about?

CHAMBERLAIN: Your Majesty, it is the simplest thing. You approach her, you smile to her, you say something, you tell her a joke—then she, of course, will have to smile, perhaps even to laugh—then you will smile back, and so on and so forth. You will start what it might be permissible to call happy social intercourse.

KING: Smile, smile. Why should I put myself out? Because she is too shy? Lord Chamberlain, you do it. (*Wants to leave.*)

CHAMBERLAIN: But, Sire, surely it isn't the first time you will have had to put a girl at ease?

KING: It's all very well, but this wretch is so scared.

CHAMBERLAIN: Everybody is a little afraid.

KING: But she is so lackadaisical about it. No guts even about being afraid, eh? So dull. Oh, here she is. Wait, now, I am not going to make a fool of myself all by myself. Don't go, stay. (*He assumes a pleasant face.*)

Enter IVONA.

Nice to see you here.

IVONA *approaches, looks around.*

(*Good-naturedly.*) Looking for something, eh?

IVONA: Wool...

KING: Wool?

IVONA: Wool...

KING: Oh, here it is. (*Laughs.*)

IVONA *takes the wool.*

Ha, ha ha.

IVONA *is silent.*

Was it lost?

IVONA *is silent.*

Hm, hm. (*Walks up to* IVONA.) What is it? What? (*Laughs.*) Well, we are a little scared? There is nothing to be scared of. Nothing at all. Eh? (*Impatiently.*) I said there's nothing to be afraid of.

IVONA *withdraws a little.*

I am father. I am Philip's father, daddy. Ugh. Not daddy, father. Anyhow, I am not a stranger. (*He comes nearer.* IVONA *withdraws farther.*) You mustn't . . . I am a plain, ordinary man. Well, not ordinary—but I am not an ogre. I have not eaten any little children. There is nothing to be afraid of. I am not a beast. I am saying I am not a beast. I am not a beast. (*Nervously.*) There is nothing to be afraid of. I am not a beast. (*Comes nearer still.* IVONA *backs away violently, drops her wool. The* KING *shouts.*) I say there is nothing to be afraid of, I am not a beast!

CHAMBERLAIN: No, no, shh . . . no.

KING: You damned bitch!

IVONA *backs out of the room.*

CHAMBERLAIN: Hush. Somebody may hear you.

KING: She is scared. Scared! Scared, my foot . . . not properly scared, just indulging herself. Mama, boo, boo, gugga.

CHAMBERLAIN: I would venture to suggest that she is not even capable of being properly afraid. Some of our ladies can be afraid beautifully, with such charm, such piquancy. This one only just manages to be scared. There is nothing to it. (*With distaste.*) No frills, the plainest possible thing.

KING: I've just remembered something . . .

CHAMBERLAIN: Remembered? What?

KING: Afraid, afraid. Lord Chamberlain, do you remember that one . . . the one we . . . a long time ago. How one forgets, eh?

CHAMBERLAIN: Whom, Your Majesty?

KING: It's a long time, I have forgotten all about it till now. I was only a Prince and you were only an embryo Chamberlain. That little one we . . . you know . . . I think on this sofa. I think she was a seamstress.

CHAMBERLAIN: The little seamstress. The sofa. Youth. Oh, blissful days of youth.

Enter CHECKERS.

What is it, Checkers? Do not interrupt.

CHECKERS *leaves.*

KING: She died soon after that, I think. Drowned herself.

CHAMBERLAIN: She did. I remember as if it were yesterday, she walked onto a bridge and then from the bridge . . . splash. Oh, youth, youth. There is nothing to equal it.

KING: Wouldn't you think she was rather like this Grumpy Dumpy?

CHAMBERLAIN: But, Your Majesty, this one is a bloated blonde and the other was a thin brunette.

KING: But she was scared in the same way. Bungle, botch —mama, gugga . . . just the same. She was scared stiff, the trollop.

CHAMBERLAIN: If these memories displease Your Majesty, it is better to forget. It's better not to remember dead women. A dead woman isn't a woman at all.

KING: She was scared and she looked ill-used—just as this one. On this sofa. Ugh, why should something always remind one of something else? I can now remember the whole damn thing.

Enter the QUEEN.

QUEEN: Congratulations! Wonderful! You have put her at her ease, you have reassured her! Paralyzed with fear, poor thing. What has got into you, Ignatius? You have spoiled everything.

KING: Hell and damnation, don't you come near me, Madame.

QUEEN: What's all this? Why shouldn't I come nearer?

KING: Why? Why? Always why. Can't I have any wishes of my own? Am I not my own master? Must I explain everything? Why are you looking at me? Why are you staring? Well, why? Why did I rage at her? Because she reminded me of something.

CHAMBERLAIN: Not worth mentioning, Your Majesty. It isn't worth telling . . .

KING: She reminded me about something, about you, if you want to know. Yes, about you, my darling.

QUEEN: About me?

KING: Ha, ha, ha. There is no need to stare. Hang it all, I am sorry. Margaret, I admit that I got carried away, but can you imagine, I can't even look at this poor child without thinking of you. I didn't want to speak about it, it is embarrassing, but if you want me to be frank, I will. You know how sometimes one person reminds us of another—not altogether, in sort of a different condition as it were, you understand? When I see Grumpy Dumpy . . . the way she has . . . sloppy, groping, fumbling—it makes me think of you. (*Whispers.*) All floppy . . . and undone.

QUEEN: She reminds you of my . . . ?

KING: Exactly. Exactly what you are thinking. Say it. Say it yourself and you will see it is the same. Whisper it to me.

QUEEN: Ignatius, my God.

KING: I see, Madame, you would rather keep your little secrets.

QUEEN: You are forgetting yourself.

KING: On the contrary, I am remembering. I am remembering all sorts of things. In a moment I shall remember all . . . Mama, gugga . . . (*Muttering.*) Remember, remember . . . (*Leaves hurriedly.*)

QUEEN: What does it all mean?

LORD CHAMBERLAIN *runs after the* KING. *The* QUEEN *remains, thoughtful. Enter* ISOBEL, *titivates herself in front of a looking glass.*

Stop titivating yourself.

ISOBEL (*ashamed*):   Your Majesty.

QUEEN: You are doing it all the time. Since this . . . this . . . unfortunate creature appeared at Court, you are all fidgeting, and preening yourselves. Come here now, girl, I must ask you something.

ISOBEL: Your Majesty.

QUEEN: Look at me. Look straight into my eyes. Admit it. You have told somebody. You have been prattling about my poems. Admit it. You couldn't keep the secret any longer and you told them.

ISOBEL: Your Majesty.

QUEEN: You haven't? If you have told nobody, how could he have found out? He must have found my notebook under the mattress.

ISOBEL: Who, Your Majesty?

QUEEN: That is it. That is what he meant. Look, tell me frankly as if I weren't the Queen. I am releasing you— temporarily of course—from all the deference due to me. Tell me the truth. When you are looking at Ivona, does anyone else come to mind? No association? The way she walks, for instance. Her nose? The way she looks, her general behavior? Does she remind you of somebody? Some affinity? Do you think that a malicious person could see some link between her and . . . and my own . . . my poetry?

ISOBEL: Your poetry? Your Majesty, how . . . What is this?

QUEEN: The disastrous, the cursed poetry. The world is far too vulgar. Disastrous ecstasies, fatal reveries, pernicious confidences. You are not telling the truth. Why did he say "floppy"? If he had not read it, he would not use the word. Are my rhymes so naked, so undone?

"Undone"—oh, horrible word. But you are not telling the truth. Swear, swear by the light of these candles. This is of the utmost gravity. Swear properly, kneel down and take an oath. Repeat after me: I swear . . .

PRINCE PHILIP *enters, followed by the* KING *and* LORD CHAMBERLAIN.

PHILIP: Mother, I would like to talk to you. But I am sorry . . . what am I interrupting? A sorcery session?

QUEEN: No, no, she is just doing up my shoes. These shoes are too large.

PHILIP: Why, pray, did the King frighten my fiancée?

QUEEN: Not this tone, Philippe.

PHILIP: What tone would you find suitable? What tone should I use when my father bullies my fiancée for no reason and treats her brutally? She is now half paralyzed with fear. I can't leave you with her for one moment without your maltreating her in any way you think fit. Under the circumstances I think I am fantastically calm.

Enter CHECKERS.

Go out, Checkers. Mother, I would like to talk to you alone.

QUEEN: I will agree to talk to you alone if you tell me first what you are going to say.

ISOBEL *retires.*

PHILIP: I see you are being cautious, Mother. Forgive me if I say something which sounds odd. I don't know how to put it. Is it true that she reminds the King of some past sin of yours?

QUEEN: Who told you?

PHILIP: Father. He told me that he had given her a scolding because she reminded him of your secret vice.

KING *and* LORD CHAMBERLAIN *enter.*

QUEEN: Ignatius, what have you been telling Philippe?

KING: Nothing, except the truth, of course. He pestered me, so I told him. Why? When? What? I told him the truth. I would much rather he pestered you than me.

QUEEN: Ignatius.

PHILIP: If only you would pay some attention to my situation: out of the blue my father assaults my fiancée. When I ask him, as I surely have a right to, why he has done it, you both start talking in riddles. Why, because of my mother's past sins, should my father let fly at my fiancée?

KING: Yes, I assaulted, I attacked, I let fly. And why, do you think, I did it? Is it because of my own little sins or somebody else's? Why are you staring, Margaret? If you stare at me, I will stare at you.

PHILIP: My parents stare at one another because of my fiancée. My mother stares at my father, my father stares at my mother, all because of my fiancée.

KING: Don't laugh at your father, Philip. And pipe down.

QUEEN: Your father was vexed and annoyed and told you the first thing that came into his mind. To stop you pestering him. It is absurd, not worth talking about. Let us change the subject.

PHILIP: Madame, I know it is absurd.

QUEEN: Let us not talk about it any more. Absolute nonsense.

PHILIP: Nonsense, indeed. Quite absurd. Idiotic. (*Bows.*)

QUEEN: Why are you bowing?

PHILIP (*confidentially*): Because where she is concerned I am a little absurd too.

QUEEN: You, absurd?

PHILIP: It is difficult to call it anything else. I do not love her, and this makes me behave like a fool. I can see why you behave stupidly toward her, because I do the same myself.

KING: Philip, you're taking liberties. Hold your tongue.

PHILIP *bows.*

Why are you bowing again, you fool? This is going too far.

PHILIP (*confidentially*): But with her one can go as far as one likes.

KING: What? What is this? As far as one likes? I wouldn't like to go anywhere with her. What is it all about? Lord Chamberlain . . .

QUEEN: Philippe, stop this bowing! Why are you doing it?

KING (*aside*): Garbage!

CHAMBERLAIN: One may be able to do anything one likes to her but that does not mean that the Prince can do anything he likes to us, does it?

The PRINCE *bows now to* LORD CHAMBERLAIN *who backs away in a panic.*

Not to me. I had nothing to do with it. Don't come near me.

PHILIP (*confidentially*): Anyone can come near her, of course. One can pull her hair, one can tweak her ear.

KING: Ha, ha, ha. (*Embarrassed, stops abruptly.*) I mean . . . you know . . . eh?

CHAMBERLAIN: Your Highness, if you touch me, I . . .

PHILIP: Anyone can touch her. Believe me, you can do absolutely anything you like with her. She is made for it—for anything. She is too shy to protest, too disagreeable. One can do anything. One can be stupid, idiotic, cynical, horrid. (*Bows to* LORD CHAMBERLAIN.) Anything you fancy, Your Excellence.

CHAMBERLAIN (*recoils*): I am not interested. It is a matter of complete indifference to me. (*Bows to* PRINCE PHILIP.) I take my leave. (*Exit.*)

KING: Garbage. Why are you staring, Philip? Good day. (*Bows.*) Good day. Out, out. (*Exit.*)

QUEEN: What do you mean? Explain, explain. Good-bye. (*Exit.*)

PHILIP (*shouts after* LORD CHAMBERLAIN, KING, *and* QUEEN): You can do anything. Everything. Whatever you like. (*To himself.*) She is still sitting somewhere and loves me. Loves me. Whatever you like, whatever you can think of. Everything. (*Notices* ISOBEL, *who has got up from a chair she has been sitting on during the preceding scene.* PRINCE *comes up to her and kisses her neck.*) You can let yourself go with her, anything goes!

ISOBEL: Let me go.

PHILIP: Oh, with her one can do just as one pleases. (*Kisses her on the lips.*) Ah, delightful.

ISOBEL (*struggling*): I will scream.

PHILIP: But I am telling you you can do as you like with her. I am sorry, I did not mean you, didn't want to, really. It just happened. I am sorry. What have I done? I have behaved like a fool again.

ISOBEL: The impertinence.

PHILIP: I beg you not to tell anyone. If my fiancée were to hear of it she would be hurt. Hurt, hurt, hurt, hurt.

ISOBEL: But let me go, Your Highness.

PHILIP (*still holding her*): In a moment . . . hurt. (*Kisses her.*) What a nose, what a lovely mouth you have. Don't go. I believe I am being unfaithful. It's terrible. It's glorious. It's easy. Checkers! Checkers!

ISOBEL (*struggling*): At least don't call anyone.

PHILIP: On the contrary, my love.

Enter CHECKERS.

Checkers, ask Master Simon to come with Miss Ivona at once.

CHECKERS *leaves*.

There is no question of my letting you go. I feel at ease at last. The delight of embracing an attractive girl. I shall send you flowers. Oh, how easy it all is. I have my touch again. I must turn it to good account. I love you.

Enter SIMON *and* IVONA.

Simon, this is my present fiancée.

SIMON: What?

PHILIP: Ivona, I must confess something to you. Just a moment ago I was unfaithful. You are no longer my fiancée. I am sorry but there is nothing I can do about it. You are not desirable and Isobel is. Do not be offended that I announce it so lightly. (*To* ISOBEL.) Everything will be easy from now on, thanks to you, my treasure, my darling. (*Kisses Isobel's hand. To* IVONA.) Why are you standing like this? Actually, you can stand as you like, it doesn't matter any more. Farewell. I am going, moving away, further and further away from you. I am breaking it off. I warn you, you won't gain anything by standing there.

SIMON: She won't gain anything. Not if she stood for ten years. What fun it all is. This is marvelous.

PHILIP (*to* ISOBEL): I am sorry, my heart, I haven't even asked if you consent. Don't refuse me. (*Kisses her hand.*) Each gesture makes me happier and healthier. I will give the necessary orders immediately. There is no need to keep our engagement secret. My parents will be pleased. The Lord Chamberlain . . . the kind Chamberlain will be delighted. The Court . . . it will be a load off everyone's mind. Really, the atmosphere was becoming impossible, I know. (*To* IVONA.) Still standing? Surely everything is straight between us. What are you waiting for, my dear?

SIMON: She won't move.

PHILIP: Call that lover of hers, let him cart her away, remove her from here to wherever it is she lives.

SIMON: I will get him at once and we will send her off. Immediately, Philip, so she doesn't gain ground by staying here.

PHILIP: Don't worry.

SIMON *leaves*.

You can stand as long as you like, you won't get me again into another absurd mess. I have changed and everything has changed with me. There you stand—a living reproach—but it means nothing to me. Stand as much as you like. Ha, ha, ha. Anyhow, you like to be hurt because you're sexless, you dislike yourself, you are your own enemy. You get the worst out of everyone. You make everyone turn against you, you make everyone feel a knave and a thief. But if you stand here for a year you can do nothing to me. I am free, everything is going to be child's play. (*Smiles lightheartedly at* IVONA *then spins* ISOBEL *around*.)

ISOBEL: Wouldn't it be better not to tell her all this? Have some pity, Philip.

PHILIP: No, no pity now. Only pleasure. I know her from experience. Above all, one must keep talking as long as she is here, one must keep telling her the worst things in the lightest possible tone. This is the point— the more unpleasant, or indecent the matter, the more innocent the manner: making light of the whole thing. In this way her very existence is discouraged, her silence not allowed to speak. She cannot put anyone under an obligation. It places her in a world where she can do nothing. Don't worry about me, I am safe now. It really is very easy to break things off, it is only a question of changing the key. Let her stand, by all means let her stand and stare. Let us go. It has not struck me before that one can simply leave her behind. If she is staying, we will go.

IVONA *stoops*.

Don't curtsy to me.

IVONA: I am not curtsying.

PHILIP: Let it go. What did you pick up? A hair? What do you want it for? It's Isobel's. Drop it.

IVONA *is silent.*

Enter SIMON *and* INNOCENT.

INNOCENT: I am sorry but you can't do this. First Your Highness made the girl fall in love with you and now you are sending her away. Royal fancy. You broke her heart. I protest.

PHILIP: Oh, you protest?

INNOCENT: Or rather, I am trying to protest. (*Sits down abruptly under Prince's threatening stare.*)

PHILIP: Look how this man sat on his protest.

SIMON: He sat on it as a dog on his tail. Off with you now—take your ladylove and off with you both. Go.

PHILIP: Wait—she must give up that hair.

SIMON: Hair, Sir?

PHILIP: Give me that hair, Ivona, do you hear?

ISOBEL: Philip, I have enough hair . . .

PHILIP: No, she must give it back. I can't stand her taking it with her. (*Recovers the hair from* IVONA.) I've got it. But that's not enough. It is not the hair—it is us, she has still got us. (*To* ISOBEL.) We are still in her, the trap. Go on, I will come in a moment. Simon.

All leave except SIMON.

Stop her from leaving the castle. Don't let her go.
Let everything appear to be just as before. For the
moment my breaking it off must not be made public.

SIMON: I knew it. I knew that she would get you again
if we let her stand.

PHILIP: I want to end it for good. Don't get alarmed. I
will have to . . . (*Makes a gesture of cutting somebody's
throat.*)

SIMON: What? Whom?

PHILIP: Ivona.

SIMON: You are only working yourself up. It's all over.
You have broken it off. We will send her home and
forget about her very existence.

PHILIP: She won't be here but—she will be somewhere.
I will be here but she will still be somewhere. Ugh . . .
no, I can't stand it. I would much rather kill her once
and for all.

SIMON: But you are cured.

PHILIP: I am, I give you my word. I have fallen in love
with Isobel. I have shaken off the sufferings of that
wretch. But she still has us involved, Isobel and me, and
she will go on—in that way she has, fumbling and
fidgeting and groping—involving us. I can't stand it.
I must kill. What if she goes away? She will carry us
with her. I know that it isn't a normal practice to kill
people. But I assure you that I am absolutely sober. I
know what I am saying, I am not exaggerating one way
or another. (*Slightly anxious.*) You must admit, I do
not even look excited, do I?

SIMON: Do you really want to kill her? You mean—kill, just like that? It is a crime, you know.

PHILIP: It will be my last extravagance, last escapade, the last fling to finish it all. I will play it light, cool, and easy—you will see. It seems terrible, but in fact it is like an operation, no more. It must be the easiest possible thing, to kill such a weakling. She is asking for it. Will you promise to help me?

SIMON: What she is making you do, the whore!

PHILIP: We will keep my engagement to Isobel secret for the moment. Don't tell anybody about it. Let everything appear as before . . . till tomorrow. Tomorrow I shall devise the most convenient method of extermination. But you must help me. I can't do it alone. I must do it with somebody. I won't do it by myself.

——————ACT FOUR

A room in the castle. Trumpets, etc. Enter the KING *followed by three* DIGNITARIES.

KING (*absentmindedly*): All right, all right. Stop pestering me. I have important matters to attend to. Anything else?

CHANCELLOR: Your Majesty has still to decide what clothes would be appropriate for the Ambassador Extraordinary and Minister Plenipotentiary we are sending to France. Should he wear Court dress or uniform?

KING (*gloomily*): Let him go stark naked.

DIGNITARIES *shocked*.

I am sorry, I am a little absentminded today. Let him go just as he likes. So long as he is paying for it himself, of course.

DIGNITARIES: This is the decision we had expected Your Majesty would take in your superior wisdom.

MARSHAL: Your Majesty, we are having tonight a great banquet to celebrate the occasion of the inspiring and

democratic betrothal of Prince Philip to the flower of the lowest social strata of our society, Miss Ivona Hopit. Has Your Majesty any special directives regarding the menu?

KING: Give 'em pigswill.

DIGNITARIES shocked.

I meant to say, of course, serve game. That's it, game will do very well. What are you staring at me for?

DIGNITARIES: This is just the decision we had expected Your Majesty would take in your superior wisdom.

SUPREME JUDGE: Your Majesty, may I humbly submit this petition, begging your clemency on behalf of old Plimsoll. It is signed by the courts of all twelve instances.

KING: Clemency be damned! Let him hang.

DIGNITARIES: Your Majesty!

KING: Hang him, I said. Why are you staring at me again? The prerogative of mercy is mine to use just as I like; I make use of it by not using it. I want that scoundrel to hang not because he is a scoundrel but because I . . . hm . . . what I want to say is that we are all scoundrels. You, I, everybody. And now stop staring at me. I have had enough of it. As from today nobody is going to be allowed to stare at me. There is far too much staring going on altogether.

DIGNITARIES: This is precisely the decision we had expected Your Majesty to make in your superior wisdom.

KING: And now, out with you. Enough of this twaddle. And don't start to wonder by any chance. As from

today nobody is going to wonder at anything. I have been too benign with you up to now. From today I shall show you who is master around here! I am going to muzzle the whole lot of you.

DIGNITARIES *bow.*

Don't bow, I forbid you. Don't you know any better than to bow? Out!

DIGNITARIES *leave in a panic, the* KING *looks around with suspicion and hides behind a sofa. Enter* LORD CHAMBER- LAIN, *looks around equally suspiciously, and starts to move furniture around in a furtive and sly manner. He pushes an armchair, turns up a corner of a carpet, dis- arranges books on the shelves, drops a plum stone on the floor. He notices the* KING.

CHAMBERLAIN: Oh!

KING: Humph . . . humph.

CHAMBERLAIN: Your Majesty?

KING: It is me all right. What the hell are you doing here?

CHAMBERLAIN: I? Nothing.

KING (*gloomily*): You're wondering why I am in this room, aren't you? Seems the fashion these days to wonder. I am hiding, you see. I am hiding. I am laying an ambush.

CHAMBERLAIN: Ambush, Sire, for whom?

KING: Nobody in particular. Ambush for fun. (*Laugh- ing.*) This room is next to the apartments of our Grumpy Dumpy. Margaret often comes here as well. (*Lamely.*) Some of their goings-on may be worth seeing, so I would like to see them for myself.

CHAMBERLAIN: See what?

KING: Margaret.

CHAMBERLAIN: Her Majesty?

KING: Her Majesty. I would like to see what she is like when she is alone. When nobody can see her. I have been living with her for so long and I really don't know anything about her. I believe she has something on her conscience, eh? Perhaps . . . perhaps she too? There is nothing she couldn't do. My head whirls when I think of it. Perhaps she is deceiving me. That's most likely—or something else; everything is possible. Everything, anything.

CHAMBERLAIN: Your Majesty . . . that sofa . . .

KING: Keep quiet, you fool. One sofa is as good as another when one wants to hide. You, Lord Chamberlain —what were you doing? What are you doing here, moving the furniture and fiddling with bits and pieces?

CHAMBERLAIN: Just to . . .

KING: Just to what, tell me. I am also here just to . . .

CHAMBERLAIN: I am doing a tour of the castle and I am trying to make things a little difficult.

KING: Difficult?

CHAMBERLAIN: For instance (*sitting down*), it is a little difficult to sit down when the chair is put this way. (*Demonstrates.*) One may sit beside it instead.

KING: Why are you dropping plum stones on the floor, Lord Chamberlain?

CHAMBERLAIN: To make it a little difficult to walk, Your Majesty.

KING: Difficult to walk? (*Gloomily.*) Aah, so she has managed to get your back up, too? Dumpy Grumpy. (*Retreating.*) It's nothing, eh?

CHAMBERLAIN: Your Majesty, I am a man of the world and of certain standing. I abhor all this impudence, this insolence, this dissipation sprouting up everywhere. If it must go on, I don't know where it will end.

KING: Yes, yes, insolence . . . getting worse. Dissipation. Eh? Do you remember, old friend? (*Nudges* LORD CHAMBERLAIN.)

CHAMBERLAIN: I don't want to remember anything, Sire.

KING: He bowed to you as well as to me, you know. It's nothing. Dissipation increasing . . . insolence . . . well, well. And what if I jump from behind the sofa as she passes and spring at her and frighten her, frighten her. One can do it to her, one can do anything to her, frighten her and strangle her—yes—kill her. We have killed one before, after all.

CHAMBERLAIN: *Fi donc*, Your Majesty!

KING: I am only telling you one can do anything with her . . . it does not matter with her. You can do just as you like.

CHAMBERLAIN: Your Majesty, this is out of the question. Heaven help us! As it is, this court is already seething with gossip and intrigue. And now, to cap it all, Your Royal Majesty popping out from behind a sofa. The need for tact and *savoir faire* has never been greater than in present circumstances. On the other hand (*laughs*), a certain solution has just occurred to me. (*Laughs.*)

KING: Why are you laughing like an idiot?

CHAMBERLAIN: This is the solution. Your Majesties are giving a banquet today to celebrate this deplorable betrothal. Now, if we served fish, fish full of bones— pike, for instance? It is in season now, one could serve it in a cream sauce.

Enter CHECKERS.

Leave.

KING (*gloomily*): Out. Pike . . .

CHAMBERLAIN: Pike. (*Laughs.*)

KING: What do you mean—pike?

CHAMBERLAIN: Your Majesty, pike served at an official banquet! I don't know whether you have noticed that she is even more lost when there are many people around? And it is so easy—yesterday I only gave her one look, a little up and down look, and she almost choked on a potato. If one were to serve pike, it is such a difficult fish to eat, so full of bones. And if one were to serve it at an official banquet, with so many people there—wouldn't it be an easy thing to choke?

KING: My Lord Chamberlain (*looks at* CHAMBERLAIN), it sounds silly. Pike?

CHAMBERLAIN (*a little hurt*): I know it sounds silly. I wouldn't be telling you about it, Sire, if it weren't.

KING (*scared*): My Lord Chamberlain, but what? If she really . . . ? Could she really choke?

CHAMBERLAIN (*haughtily*): Then Your Majesty believes that she could really . . . But that would be so silly, didn't you say? And if by mere chance such a silly

accident did occur, what could we possibly have to do with . . . such silliness?

KING: But didn't we? Didn't we talk about it?

CHAMBERLAIN: Oh, that was just talk . . . (*Looks attentively at his nails.*)

KING: Just talk? Ha, it can be done. I know how to do it. If we storm her from above, we attack her sharply enough, we can get away with anything, even a plan so silly that nobody would suspect us. Why not carp? It shall be carp, Lord Chamberlain.

CHAMBERLAIN: Pike, pike.

KING: But why not carp? Or eel? I suppose, pike will do from above . . . Hm . . . (*Scared again.*) Storm her from above?

CHAMBERLAIN: Yes, indeed, Your Majesty. Charging at her in full regalia.

KING: Yes, yes, full regalia, of course, plenty of light, lots of people and magnificent clothes. Splendor, grandeur, and glory, then one battle cry from above and she's had it. She will choke to death for sure. And nobody will be any the wiser because it is too silly. We will do it in the grand manner, bear down on her from on high, not from beneath. Royally we'll kill her, eh? I can see the Queen, let's hide.

CHAMBERLAIN: But . . .

KING: Let's hide, I want to have a look at her.

They hide behind the sofa. The QUEEN *comes in holding a little bottle.*

(*Aside.*) What's that? (*Sticks his head out.*)

CHAMBERLAIN: Ssh...

> QUEEN walks a few steps toward Ivona's room, stops, takes out a little book, groans quietly, and covers her face with her hand.

KING (aside): What is this? A book of grief?

CHAMBERLAIN (aside): Ssh...

QUEEN (reads out): I am alone. (Repeats.) Yes, I am alone, alone. Nobody knows, oh, oh. (Reads.)

> To you, my little notebook's reams
> I trust my reveries and dreams
> My chaste thoughts are here for you
> Nobody guesses that this is true.

(Speaks.) Nobody guesses, indeed! How terrible it is. How terrible. O death. (Lifts up a little bottle.) O poison.

KING (aside): Poison?

QUEEN (her face contorted with grief): Let nobody guess. Let us read on. Let these words strengthen our determination to do the terrible deed. (Reads.)

> My people, you see me on the throne,
> You see me when my crown is on,
> You do not know what fumbles inside,
> Perhaps you think it's only pride.
> In fact in that too rich a frame
> I grope toward another name.
> Undone within, royal outside,
> I would rather be a floppy bride.
> I want to be free as a bird on the wing
> So that my verses may better sing.

Oh, suppleness, floppiness. Oh, I must burn this. Destroy it. It's terrifying. And I wrote it. It's mine and whatever happens it still is mine. Oh, I see now the whole horror of it. Ignatius, Ignatius has read it. I see the likeness . . . I do . . . as she slobbers, gropes, stumbles. She is herself a terrifying allusion to my poetry. She is the informer, the betrayer. It's me, it's me, it's mine. There is a likeness between us. Oh, how she has dragged it all out into the open. How she has exposed it. Anyone who has seen her will discover that likeness to Margaret. Anyone who looks at her will know me as I really am just as if he read my most intimate lines. Enough. She must perish. Margaret, Margaret, you have to put her to death. Forward, murderous bottle. She must not continue on this earth, there is no time left—otherwise everyone will know about that poisonous link between us. I don't wish to become the butt of ridicule, gossip, and derision, the scapegoat of aggression. To death with her. Let us go quietly to her room and put a few drops from this bottle into her medicine. Nobody will know. She is such a weakling, they will think she has just died. Who could guess it was me? I am the Queen. (*Moves on.*) No, I can't go like this. I can't look my ordinary self when I am about to do murder. I must change, get my hair disheveled at least, not too much, nothing ostentatious, just enough to effect a change. Like this.

KING (*aside*): Ssh . . .

QUEEN: Shall I go so disheveled? But that may betray you. If anybody should catch you with your hair all over the place. Stop talking to yourself. I am sure she also talks to herself. Margaret, stop talking to yourself. It may give you away. (*Looks into a mirror.*) This

glass is showing me up. I can't go like this. I must bring all my ugliness into the open before I am ready to go. Stop talking to yourself. Somebody will hear you. I can't stop talking to myself. Do all murderers talk to themselves before the act? There is something odd, abnormal about this room—a sort of venomous disorder? A twisted mouth, Margaret, that's what is needed. That's better, let's go now. You and I together. But am I not going alone? Twist your mouth more. Let us go. Remember all your lines and go. Remember all your pliable reveries and go. Remember the suppleness, the secret striving suppleness and go. I am going. I can't . . . it is too insane. A moment longer, let us put on a little smear . . . the ink here (smears some ink on her face). Now it's going to be much easier . . . I am different. Stop, this may betray you. Let us go, to kill the informer. Let us read the poem again, just a moment longer (takes out her book of poems), to inflame the desire to murder.

KING (jumps up): Margaret!

QUEEN: Ignatius . . .

KING: I have caught you, red-handed. Show it to me. (Wants to take her book.)

QUEEN: Let me go!

KING: Let me see it! Now, oh, murderess. I want to see all your secret sins. Let me see and we shall start another honeymoon. Let me see, you secret poisoner.

QUEEN: Ah. (Faints.)

CHAMBERLAIN: Water, water. She has fainted.

KING: Ha. Now we know. She dreams of suppleness and

wants to poison Grumpy Dumpy. It doesn't matter anyhow. I have killed her already.

QUEEN (*faintly*):   You killed her? Whom?

KING: I have drowned her. I and our Chamberlain. We have drowned her together.

CHAMBERLAIN: Water. Here is some water.

QUEEN: You have drowned . . . Ivona?

KING: Silly. Not Ivona, but it makes no difference. Not Ivona, another one. Long time ago. Now you know about me. You know? Compared to my crimes, all your silly little verses are just nothing. I have killed her and now I will kill Grumpy Dumpy. I will kill her too.

QUEEN: You will kill . . .

KING: Yes, now I will kill her. If it comes off. Someone is doing it to someone else somewhere every minute of the day. All the time, if not this one then another. And if not that one, somebody else. You know— charging from above with full regalia, and then . . . (*To* CHAMBERLAIN.) Give me some water. (*Drinks.*) I am old . . . I am getting older.

QUEEN: I won't let you, Ignatius. I forbid it.

KING: You will let me, dearie, you will, as you let yourself, as everyone lets everyone else.

Enter IVONA, *wants to withdraw when she sees the others, but is unable to do it and proceeds to her room. From this moment everyone talks in whispers.*

KING: Ha!

QUEEN: Ignatius, I don't agree, I don't want you to . . .

CHAMBERLAIN: Quiet, for goodness' sake.

KING: Be quiet, you fool. (To CHAMBERLAIN.) It will be all right. (To QUEEN.) Do you think I would do it the way you planned, from beneath? Not on your life. I will kill her in style, in majesty, with a battle cry and yet so stupidly that nobody will be any the wiser. Margaret, a murder has to be highhanded and not done meekly, cap in hand. Go and wash yourself, you are looking a sight. And get that banquet going. It is getting late. We will have pike for the hors d'oeuvre by the way. I would like pike myself, in a cream sauce. Very good fish, pike. Special. Eh?

QUEEN: Pike . . . ? Pike? (To LORD CHAMBERLAIN.) He has gone mad. Thank God.

KING: Hold your tongue. I haven't gone mad. Give us pike as I tell you.

CHAMBERLAIN: Madame, pike makes an excellent hors d'oeuvre. I can't see any reason why one shouldn't serve pike.

QUEEN: I am not going to serve pike. Don't drive me out of my mind. I am not going to serve anything of the sort. Why pike? It's unheard of, the whole thing. Why should I serve pike?

KING: What temper! (To CHAMBERLAIN.) Give me the crown. (Puts it on.)

QUEEN (terrified): Ignatius! Take it off, Ignatius.

KING: Margaret, if I tell you to serve pike you will serve pike. Don't bicker or I will crown you. I can crown you. I can crown you for I am a sinner. I can do any-

thing and you tremble before me for I am a sinner. I am the king of sin, get that, I am the king of rot and sin, of rape and groans.

QUEEN (terrified): Ignatius!

KING: Oh, well. Now, now. Serve pike. Invite all the elderly statesmen, all those old experienced intimidators, you know, the old boys who would paralyze the devil himself with fright. (In a lower voice.) Margaret, enough of all this shyness, fear, shame, do you understand? Enough poetry, flexibility, pliability. You are not a chick, you are a lady, the Queen. You should not flop, the others have to bend, not you, remember. Now go and wash yourself, you are looking like nothing on earth, you slattern. Put on your damask dress— show what you can do, dearie. Get a move on. Pull yourself together—a gracious bearing and tact and a royal manner—general refinement is your style, after all. Tell your wenches to put on their best front too. Now, get going. You understand? You have to put on a first class performance, you and your women—they are to be ladies and not sluts. Assemble the guests and order the food and don't bother about the rest, I will deal with that. Remember—grandly, grandly, royally. One, two, three—majesty. Now go, you slave.

The QUEEN, covering her face with her hands, leaves.

Lord Chamberlain . . . (Nudges him.)

CHAMBERLAIN: Sire?

KING (whispering gloomily): Bow to me. I need you to bow.

CHAMBERLAIN (listening): Somebody is coming.

KING: We'd better hide.

They hide behind the sofa. Enter, creeping, PHILIP, *carrying a knife, followed by* SIMON, *carrying a basket.*

PHILIP: Where has she gone?

SIMON: Ssh, here.

PHILIP: What is she doing?

SIMON (*looking into Ivona's room*):   Swatting flies.

PHILIP: Swatting?

SIMON: Yawning.

PHILIP (*getting his knife ready*):   Let us try. One, two, three. See that nobody is coming. Get your basket ready.

SIMON opens the basket, PHILIP *creeps toward Ivona's door.*

KING (*aside to* LORD CHAMBERLAIN):   Our Phil is at it as well.

CHAMBERLAIN: Ssh.

SIMON (*who has been observing* PHILIP):   Philip, stop. Or I will give the alarm.

PHILIP: Nervous?

SIMON: It's impossible. Going for that wretch with a knife. It's too silly—one can't do it. You can't knife somebody like that. And the basket.

PHILIP: Stop! (*Puts the knife down.*) Technically, the basket is indispensable.

SIMON: If only you could see yourself.

PHILIP: Enough.

SIMON (*looking again into Ivona's room*):   Going to sleep. May be asleep now . . .

PHILIP: Asleep?

SIMON: It looks like it. She is lolling in her chair.

PHILIP (*looking in*): Now or never. If now, it would be painless. You try.

SIMON: Me?

PHILIP: It's easier for you. You are a stranger and an equal. You are not her target—she does not love you. Simon, do it for me. It won't take more than a second. It's an operation—she won't feel a thing. She won't even know that in the same second that you do it, she won't exist any more. It will happen outside her, it is so easy, it is our act and it does not concern her really.

SIMON: This ease makes it hard to do. (*Takes the knife.*)

PHILIP: No, no, no.

SIMON: No?

PHILIP: It is as if you were about to slaughter a hen.

SIMON: Can't we? I had thought we could but we can't. Damn it! She is too weak, too sickly. If only she were a stout, red-cheeked wench—but she is so pale. One can't do it to one so pale, can one?

PHILIP: Somebody is watching us.

SIMON: I am watching.

PHILIP: No, it's somebody else—who sees everything.

SIMON: I see it, of course.

PHILIP: Yes, you see me and I see you. You better go now, I prefer to be on my own. I will deal with it. An operation, rather horrid perhaps, but still an operation. I would rather be a monster for a moment than for a lifetime. Go behind the door, I will do it (*Exit* SIMON.) On my own. It really is salvation for her, isn't it? The end of suffering. And for me as well. The whole thing is perfectly rational. (*Looks around, picks up the knife, puts it down again.*) Simon!

KING (*aside, very excited*):   You are a bungler.

SIMON: Yes? (*Returns.*)

PHILIP: It is even worse on one's own. The thing looms so large . . . swelling and growing horribly. What's that?

SIMON: She is breathing . . .

They both listen.

PHILIP: Breathing. (*Looks into Ivona's room.*) Breathing, alive, all of her together, in herself, up to her eyes, immersed, contained in herself. (*Takes the knife.*) Easy enough to push this into the flesh . . . but the problem is still there. Unresolved. It is too easy and it will come to nothing.

Enter ISOBEL.

ISOBEL: What is this? (*At the sight of the knife.*) Murder?

PHILIP *and* SIMON: Ssh . . .

ISOBEL: Murder . . . would'st thou be a murderer?

PHILIP: Keep quiet and don't interfere. I am settling a few personal matters and I shall join you when I am ready. Go now.

ISOBEL (*to* SIMON): You too? Are you the accomplice?

SIMON: It's mad, Philip. Let's leave it.

KING (*aside*): Mad, indeed.

ISOBEL: Come away, I beseech you.

PHILIP (*looking into Ivona's room*): Asleep.

ISOBEL: Let her sleep. What is that to you that she is asleep? I too will sleep . . . tonight, Philip.

PHILIP: Ssh. A sigh.

ISOBEL: I too will sigh . . . tonight. Don't think of her, don't murder her. Come away, Philip.

PHILIP: Dreaming, what dreams?

ISOBEL: Let her be. I will tell you of my dream last night. I dreamed of you. Come, please.

PHILIP: About me, about us. She must be dreaming about us. About you and me. You and I are in there.

ISOBEL: In there? In what?

PHILIP: In her, inside, within. Don't you hear she is in pain, painfully asleep? Her breathing sounds cruel. It must be hard labor, with the two of us. She will be trying all sorts of things; she will let herself go. I wonder what she is up to now.

ISOBEL: You are not yourself, Philip. You have lost touch again.

PHILIP (*still whispering*): I am myself but how can I be myself, how can I get back to norm if she stays outside it? And from outside she plays the tune and we dance. She calls the tune and we dance to it. Tra-la-la, tra-la-la.

ISOBEL: How can you, Philip, after what happened between us? Don't you remember last night?

PHILIP (*listening*): Snoring.

ISOBEL: What?

PHILIP: Snoring.

ISOBEL: This really is too much.

KING: Too much, damn it. Get on! Over and done with!

PHILIP (*answering without realizing it*): I can't. What is this? Who said that? Have you noticed? There is something odd about this room. Look at the furniture. (*Knocks over a chair.*)

KING: Odd, huh, odd.

CHAMBERLAIN: Ssh.

SIMON: Let's kill her now or let's go. I really can't stand here forever with this basket. I will go, I will run away from here. I won't be an accessory any longer.

PHILIP: I must, I must.

KING: On with it, man.

ISOBEL: Kiss me. (*To* SIMON.) Make him kiss me.

PHILIP (*listening*): She's gurgling.

ISOBEL: I have had enough. I am going.

SIMON: Your Highness, do kiss her. For heaven's sake do something to make him kiss you.

KING: Go on, kiss her.

CHAMBERLAIN: Ssh.

ISOBEL: I am not going to beg for a kiss. I am not going to stand for hours outside the door of that wretch with a basket and a knife. It is too much. I leave you forever.

PHILIP (*desperately*):   Don't leave me, Isobel. I will kiss you. Wait.

ISOBEL (*pushing him away*):   I won't. Let me go. I won't kiss to order. Outside this door, with this basket, with this knife. I won't. I am going and going for good.

KING (*still behind the sofa*):   Go on. Get on with it.

PHILIP: Keep cool or we will all go crazy. Be quiet and don't wake her up. A little patience, Isobel, you are too impetuous. I mustn't lose you. Don't bother about my not being myself, I agree that one should not really kiss in these circumstances, outside this door, but let us. Let us kiss one another as if it were the most natural thing to do. If we can't be ourselves let us at least pretend we are, otherwise we shall never escape. A kiss now will be our salvation, it will bring us back to norm, it will get us out of this hole, I am sure. (*Embraces* ISOBEL.) I love you. Say that you love me.

ISOBEL: I won't. I won't say it for anything. Let me go.

PHILIP: She loves me. I love her.

IVONA *appears at the door rubbing her eyes. The* KING, *excited, leans out from behind the sofa and is held down by the* CHAMBERLAIN.

KING: Go on, Philip.

ISOBEL: Philip . . .

PHILIP (*passionately, directing her*): Philip. Philip, I love you.

SIMON: Philip, she is awake.

KING (*loudly*): Now, Philip, now. Go ahead. Give it to her. Down with Grumpy Dumpy.

CHAMBERLAIN: Hold the King.

ISOBEL: Let us run.

KING: Don't scream. Get me out of here. (*Scrambles out.*) Ugh, I am stiff, I have got pins and needles. (*To* PHILIP.) Go on. Quick. Don't botch it in the end. We will bump her off, it's now or never. This way, Chamberlain. We are off.

Enter the QUEEN *dressed for the banquet. The* FOOTMEN *bring in the lights and the tables laid for the feast. They are followed by the* GUESTS.

Wait. This is no good. We forgot the pike. Of course, from above, not from below. From on high, not cap in hand. Grandly, in majesty! Intimidate and overwhelm! Margaret, it's your turn, bear down on her. (*To the* GUESTS.) Delighted . . . delighted . . . how kind . . . straighten your tie, Philip, and straighten your hair. Royally, imperially, my son. (*To* CHAMBERLAIN.) Give me the crown.

PHILIP: What is all this?

CHAMBERLAIN: Nothing. It is only the banquet.

KING (*to the* GUESTS): Let me greet you all. Come in. Come in.

GUESTS: Your Majesty.

QUEEN: Come in. We are delighted.

GUESTS: Your Majesty. (*Bow and curtsy.*)

KING (*to the* GUESTS): And now, down to it. Let the superior gnaw at the inferior and the inferior at the superior—or rather let the superior draw out of the inferior the rightful pride and the inferior from the superior—the stimulus and the incentive to the more fruitful efforts and the noble rivalry and finally in conclusion I would just like to ask you to place my future daughter-in-law opposite us, as it is indeed in her honor that we are giving this *fête champêtre*.

The GUESTS *bow and curtsy.*

QUEEN: Whether you will sit high or low, let everybody flourish and shine in the sunlight of our graciousness. Let the ladies show themselves at their best, let the men surpass themselves. Let us all be brilliant, elegant, distinguished, and altogether remarkable.

KING: Indeed. In full dress. Forward march! Let us sit down, of course.

GUESTS: Your Majesty. (*Bow and curtsy.*)

KING *and* QUEEN *sit down.*

CHAMBERLAIN (*to* IVONA): Be gracious enough to take your seat, Madame.

IVONA *does not budge.*

Will you be so kind as to sit down. (*Puts* IVONA *on the chair.*) Your Highness, will you come here? And Your Eminence? And Your Excellency? And you, Countess Dowager? And you, kind sir?

All sit down.

KING: As we have said, we are giving this modest but elegant entertainment to celebrate the violent end . . . I mean, the happy betrothal of our future daughter-in-law. We have decided that it would be fitting to grace the occasion by bestowing upon her the title of the Princess of Burgundia, *in partibus infidelium*, of course. She is the center of tonight's festivities. Look how nicely she acknowledges it all.

GUESTS: Your Majesty. (*Discreet clapping.*)

KING (*serving himself*):   A little bony perhaps, but tasty, I think.

QUEEN (*serving herself*):   Getting on a little but very, very distinguished, I think, especially in this sauce. I find distinction much more important than what is normally described as poetry, don't you? Perhaps I am not sentimental enough but I really can't stand (*very grandly*) all that poetic diction—birds, songs, and the rest of it. It is all too, too childish and I much prefer truly mature pursuits becoming to a lady of my position, a lady *pur sang*.

GUESTS: Your Majesty.

CHAMBERLAIN (*serving himself*):   This fish looks fairly ordinary at the first glance, but how truly aristocratic it is in its very essence. What a splendid sauce. It's like cream and yet different and so superior. The taste is piquant, sharp, brilliant, paradoxical, and paradisial. I don't doubt that this distinguished gathering will do it justice.

GUESTS: Sire.

KING (*to* IVONA):   Don't you like it? (*Threatening.*) Don't you?

CHAMBERLAIN (*icily*): You must be suffering from a singular lack of appetite, Madame.

GUESTS (*shocked*): Oh.

IVONA *starts eating.*

KING (*gloomily to* IVONA): If you are not careful with this fish you might choke. Those things happen, you know. A pike like this seems innocent enough but sometimes . . .

CHAMBERLAIN (*to* IVONA): As His Majesty has just been kind enough to observe, one should be careful when eating pike or one may choke. (*Sharply.*) It's dangerous. It's a difficult fish.

KING (*menacingly*): Dangerous, I say.

GUESTS (*amazed*): Oh. (*They stop eating. Silence.*)

QUEEN (*elegantly*): *Eh, bien, Yvonne, vous ne mangez pas, ma chère?*

CHAMBERLAIN (*fixing his monocle*): You despise it? The pike of His Majesty is not good enough for you?

KING (*more menacing still*): What does this behavior mean?

IVONA *starts eating alone.*

(*Gets up, points menacingly to* IVONA.) She has choked. A bone in her throat. A bone, I say. No . . .

IVONA *chokes.*

GUESTS (*terrified, stand up*): Help. Water. Thump her on the back.

QUEEN: Help.

GUESTS: Oh, the unfortunate maid. What a thing. Catastrophe. Kaput. Dead. Dead. Let us not disturb Their Majesties . . . the family. (*They leave, exposing the body to full view.*)

PHILIP: Dead?

CHAMBERLAIN: Choked on a bone.

PHILIP: Bone? Ah, yes, a bone. I see. She looks dead enough.

Silence.

QUEEN (*nervous, perhaps slightly embarrassed*): Ignatius, we must start thinking about the Court mourning. You haven't got a suitable suit. You have put on weight and they are all too small.

KING: I haven't, have I? Well, I will order one.

QUEEN: Yes, but you must send for the tailor right away.

KING (*surprised*): Tailor? Yes, of course. (*Rubs his eyes.*) Yes, Solomon the Tailor, men's outfitters. (*Looks at* IVONA.) Dead? I mean—really dead?

QUEEN (*after a moment*): We shall all die.

KING (*after another moment*): Do something. One must do something. One must say something, surely. To deal with the silence. So, Philip, you must be brave. She is dead. You can't help it.

QUEEN (*patting* PHILIP *on the head*): Your mother is with you, son.

PHILIP: What are you saying?

CHAMBERLAIN (*to the* SERVANTS, *pointing to the body*): Take it and put it on the bed. Run, one of you, and

get the bed ready. Get Cadaver at once, the funeral director. We can't do without him. He is our key man in this. Go and get him.

The SERVANTS *draw nearer to the body.*

Wait, I will kneel. (*Kneels down.*)

KING: Yes, of course. (*Kneels down.*) This is the right thing. One should kneel.

They all kneel down except PHILIP.

We should have done it immediately.

PHILIP: Excuse me. What are you doing?

CHAMBERLAIN: What are we doing? (PHILIP *is silenced.*) Will you please kneel?

QUEEN: Kneel, Philippe. All should be kneeling. And we all are.

KING: Get down. You can't stand up, when we are all on our knees.

The PRINCE *kneels.*

1170

71 85 G   Y7 1